Think
Critically

Sara Miller McCune founded SAGE Publishing in 1965 to support the dissemination of usable knowledge and educate a global community. SAGE publishes more than 1000 journals and over 800 new books each year, spanning a wide range of subject areas. Our growing selection of library products includes archives, data, case studies and video. SAGE remains majority owned by our founder and after her lifetime will become owned by a charitable trust that secures the company's continued independence.

Los Angeles | London | New Delhi | Singapore | Washington DC | Melbourne

SUPER
QUICK
SKILLS

Think
Critically

Tom
Chatfield

Los Angeles | London | New Delhi
Singapore | Washington DC | Melbourne

Los Angeles | London | New Delhi
Singapore | Washington DC | Melbourne

SAGE Publications Ltd
1 Oliver's Yard
55 City Road
London EC1Y 1SP

SAGE Publications Inc.
2455 Teller Road
Thousand Oaks, California 91320

SAGE Publications India Pvt Ltd
B 1/I 1 Mohan Cooperative Industrial Area
Mathura Road
New Delhi 110 044

SAGE Publications Asia-Pacific Pte Ltd
3 Church Street
#10-04 Samsung Hub
Singapore 049483

Editor: Jai Seaman
Editorial assistant: Lauren Jacobs
Production editor: Ian Antcliff
Marketing manager: Catherine Slinn
Design: Shaun Mercier
Typeset by: C&M Digitals (P) Ltd, Chennai, India
Printed in the UK

© Tom Chatfield

First published 2020

Library of Congress Control Number: 2019944213

British Library Cataloguing in Publication data

A catalogue record for this book is available from
the British Library

ISBN 978-1-5264-9740-6 (pbk)

At SAGE we take sustainability seriously. Most of our products are printed in the UK using responsibly
sourced papers and boards. When we print overseas we ensure sustainable papers are used as
measured by the PREPS grading system. We undertake an annual audit to monitor our sustainability.

Contents

Everything in this book!

Section 1   What's so special about thinking critically?

It's about avoiding uncritical thinking. Don't assume the first thing you hear is true! First, you pause. Then, you try to work out what's actually happening.

Section 2   How can I make time for all this thinking?

You need to look at your habits: how you spend your time and attention, and what it means to engage effectively with things that matter.

Section 3   What do people mean when they talk about reasoning?

They're talking about how we can investigate the reasons behind things, and ask *why* and *how* they happened – rather than offering unsupported claims.

Section 4   What does a good argument look like?

When it comes to thinking critically, making a good argument means using rigorous reasoning to support a particular conclusion.

Section 5   What does a good explanation do?

Good explanations convincingly answer this question: how did the thing we're interested in come to be the way it is?

Section 6   What about bad arguments and bad explanations?

At root, bad reasoning tends to rely either on faulty assumptions or on making incorrect connections between ideas.

Section 7   Isn't everyone biased?

Yes. But this doesn't mean we're equally biased, or biased about the same things. And there's plenty we can do about our biases.

Section 8   How can I spot bias and misinformation?

It's important to compare different sources and perspectives, to know who you can trust – and to look into the stories behind each claim.

Section 9   How can I handle information overload?

Used well, technology is your friend – so long as you focus on knowledge and understanding over gathering information for its own sake.

Section 10   What do I do next?

If you can look honestly at your own habits, ideas and hopes, you'll be able to put in place a plan for progress.

What's so special about thinking critically?

10 second summary

It's not about criticizing people or sounding clever. It's about getting to grips with the real world, putting ideas to a meaningful test – and not letting others think for you.

60 second summary

Uncritical thinking can be dangerous!

Uncritically accepting everything other people tell you is a bad idea. Just imagine if you automatically believed everything you were told by every politician, advertiser or celebrity.

Critical thinking is the opposite of this kind of unthinking acceptance. It's about pausing, thinking twice, and trying to work out what is really going on.

You can't pause and think twice about everything. But when something is tricky or really matters, it's important to know how to evaluate what you're being told – or to get hold of good information.

This book is about the skills and habits that will help you do this.

How confident are you in your own thinking?

A student told us...

'I kept being told I had to think critically, make arguments and evaluate evidence – but nobody told me how to start doing it. Actually, it's a kind of common sense. You just take things slow and start thinking, step by step.'

Argument Using **reasoning,** in the form of a **premise** or linked **premises,** to try to persuade someone that they should accept the truth of a **conclusion.** An argument is thus an attempt at persuasion through reasoning.

Premise In an argument, premises are the claims that support the **conclusion**. For an argument to succeed, its premises need to form a convincing line of reasoning. An argument can have only one premise – or many. The key point is that, taken together, they should demonstrate the conclusion is correct.

Rate your confidence from one to ten in each category, where one is least and ten is most confident.

1   I know what someone means when they talk about critical thinking. .... /10

2   I can make the time to think about things that matter. .... /10

3   I can offer good reasons for my own beliefs. .... /10

4   I can understand other people's reasoning. .... /10

5   I know what it means to explain something well. .... /10

6   I can tell the difference between good and bad reasoning. .... /10

7   I understand the ideas of bias and objectivity. .... /10

8   I'm good at spotting biased or inaccurate claims. .... /10

9   I'm confident doing online research and using technology in my work. .... /10

10 I know what my priorities are for learning and improving. .... /10

TOTAL   /100

You'll probably have noticed that these questions match the ten chapters in this book, as well as giving you an overall score out of 100. If you scored over 80 – well done! If you scored under 40 – that's fine, but there's plenty of room for improvement.

Use the individual scores to prioritize your work. Spend extra time on any chapter for which you've scored yourself five or less – and ask yourself how you'd re-score yourself once you've finished it.

You'll be asked to do this self-assessment quiz again at the end of the book, to check both how you've improved overall and what your **priorities** are for further study.

This kind of reflection is itself one of the most important aspects of critical thinking. You're learning to *think about thinking itself*, a skill known as **metacognition.** The point is not to become excessively self-critical – but rather to be honest about your own strengths and weaknesses, and then to put in place a strategy to deal with these (and to keep learning).

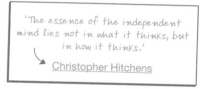

'The essence of the independent mind lies not in what it thinks, but in how it thinks.'

Christopher Hitchens

Know your strengths

Having thought about some of the areas you want to improve, it's time to think about the positive side of things: your strengths and talents.

These can be anything at all. They should simply reflect what you feel about your own thinking – and help you identify those abilities that will drive your learning and progress.

1   As a thinker, I'm good at ....

....

....

....

2   And I have a talent for ....

....

....

....

3   As well as enjoying ....

....

....

....

How can I make time for all this thinking?

10 second summary

A few simple techniques for taking control of your time and shutting out distractions will make all the difference. Above all, if something matters, give it your undivided attention.

Attention is precious: spend it wisely

Paying attention to anything takes time and energy. If you're tired, rushed or distracted, it's difficult to think carefully.

Given how many distractions there are in the world, it's vital to have a strategy for spending your time well. This means deciding on your priorities, then finding a way to focus on them.

Try to create a few hours each day when you're logged out of social media, not multitasking, and can give your full attention to the tasks or questions that matter most. Don't let your inbox turn into a to-do list written for you by other people.

Make a habit of thinking well

Willpower is less important than habit when it comes to getting things done. It's okay to be distracted sometimes – so long as you manage to find some high quality time for tasks that matter. It's also okay not to get everything done, so long as you have clear **priorities**. This means distinguishing between:

- **Urgent** things – that you need to get out of the way fast.

- **Important** things – that you need to keep working at over time.

- Things that are **neither urgent nor important**, and which can thus wait until they become urgent or important – or until you have enough free time.

- Things that are both **urgent and important** – which you ought to be getting on with *right now*!

Take control of your time

Here's a list of tactics for taking control of your time. First, **your surroundings matter**:

1 **Create a calm, uncluttered workspace** – put anything unnecessary out of sight. Depending on what works for you, use a library or study space to find focus.

Ensure your **habits** help you beat distraction – but don't assume you can focus all day. Aim for short, sharp bursts of concentration. You can achieve a great deal in even half an hour.

2 Trying '**batching**' similar tasks in bursts: an hour for email in the morning, for example, and an hour in the afternoon. Don't be constantly multitasking.

3 **Log out of social media** and shut background tabs. Set
   notifications to 'pull', meaning that you check them in bulk when
   you're ready to deal with them, rather than letting a constant 'push'
   of messages interrupt you.

4 **Try turning your phone off** or putting it into Do Not Disturb mode
   for half an hour of deep focus. You may feel very different if you
   know you can't be contacted.

It's also useful to think about your **daily rhythms** – and your best and
worst times for working.

5 Try to work out when your most **alert, productive time** of day is –
   and use it for the most important tasks.

6 Be honest about when you're most likely to be **tired and depleted** –
   and give yourself a break, or do something relaxing.

7 **Recovery** is as important as work, so make sure you keep
   boundaries around your studies. Remember that enjoyable activity
   (a passion or hobby) can be as reinvigorating as rest.

Finally, ensure you're tapping into **other people's ideas**, trying **new things**, and **not stuck in a pattern** that isn't working.

8. Set up a **study group,** or find a way to talk about what you're doing with some peers, so you can work through ideas and challenges together on a regular basis.

9. If you're getting stuck, frustrated or bothered – **make a change**. Get up, go for a walk, talk to someone, get food. Break the pattern, put yourself in a new situation.

10. **Experiment**. Try different things, find out what helps you focus and recharge – then follow whatever gets you thinking, excited and wanting to find out more.

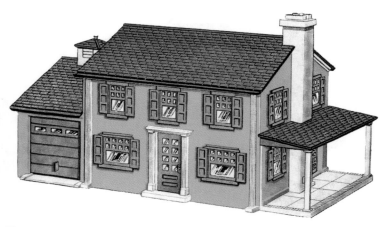

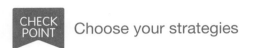

CHECK POINT Choose your strategies

Look through the list above, and pick the three tactics that are most likely to be useful for you.

1 ....

2 ....

3 ....

Now, ask yourself why you picked these. When are you going to start using them?

Make a plan. Start with the first one tomorrow, the second the next day, and the third the day after that.

A student told us...

'It's one thing being told what you ought to do, but it's different trying to actually do it. You have to look at your life, be honest with yourself, then work out what change actually means.'

'Hofstadter's Law: It always takes longer than you expect, even when you take into account Hofstadter's Law.'

Douglas Hofstadter

23

What do people mean when they talk about reasoning?

10 second summary

Reasoning is all about identifying the reasons behind things – which in turn can help us have constructive disagreements, clarify our own thinking, and change our minds.

Reason is a powerful thing

If someone asserts that something is true without offering any reasons, you don't have many options in response beyond accepting or rejecting what they've said.

But if you can persuade them to offer some reasoning in support of their claim, this changes. Now, it's possible for you to see *why* they think their claim is true. This means you can investigate whether you find their reasoning convincing (or not) – and compare it to your own.

As long as everyone is prepared to spell out their reasoning, it's even possible you'll all learn something – and come up with a more reasonable position, together, than you could alone.

It all begins with charity

A student told us...

'I've realised that, a lot of the time, people disagree because they're not even talking about the same thing. Getting people to stop shouting and start actually listening to each other, that's the problem.'

The **principle of charity** is the counter-intuitive idea that you should always try to be as generous as possible when considering ideas that you don't agree with – and should try to engage with the strongest possible form of others' reasoning.

Why? This isn't just about being polite. Instead, it enables several important things.

- It helps ensure that your own beliefs have passed the most rigorous possible test.

- It gives you the best opportunity to learn from those you disagree with.

- It maximises the chance that, if it turns out you're mistaken or don't know something, you will either change your mind or improve your reasoning.

Principle of charity
The principle that you should engage with the strongest form of other people's ideas and arguments, rather than assuming they're wrong or misguided. This helps you learn as much as possible from others, and perhaps persuade them – as opposed to setting up a **straw man** in the form of a deliberately absurd misrepresentation of someone else's ideas.

- It's much more likely to persuade those you disagree with than dismissing them.

- It allows you, and others following the same approach, to collaborate and to improve your collective understanding over time.

Don't be a straw man!

'People do not like to think. If one thinks, one must reach conclusions. Conclusions are not always pleasant.'

Helen Keller

You may have heard the phrase **a straw man** being used in politics, or elsewhere, to describe what happens when someone caricatures an opponent's beliefs in order to defeat them.

For example, in a debate about crime, someone might say 'my opponent clearly believes that thieves should be rewarded for their crimes!' in an attempt to make their opponent look ridiculous and lose support. This is known as 'building a straw man' because it involves coming up with a ridiculous, simplified version of somebody else's point of view purely so that you can destroy it – as if you were throwing a straw man onto a bonfire.

Burning straw men may be effective in politics (and social media), but it also replaces a reasoned debate with an exercise in point-scoring. Nobody is going to persuade their opponent to change their mind like this – and nobody is going to learn very much from insultingly misrepresenting someone else's ideas. In fact, it's more likely to make people abandon reasoned debate entirely and just hurl abuse at each other.

If, instead, you start off by assuming that someone else is reasonable and their views are worth taking seriously, you keep alive the prospect of constructive disagreement and debate. And if it turns out you deeply disagree with them, you're much more likely to be able to offer a convincing critique and alternative.

This is how scientific knowledge progresses (at least in theory): new evidence or insights gradually lead people to reconsider their previous beliefs.

Charity in action

Here's an exercise in applying the principle of charity. Write down an idea you disagree with.

....

Now see if you can come up with two strong reasons that someone else might have for agreeing with this idea.

1 ....

....

....

2 ....

....

....

Finally, write out the strongest objections you can come up with to these two reasons.

1 ....

....

2 ....

....

....

Congratulations

You're getting to grips with **<u>reasoning</u>**.

What's one thing that has **surprised you** or **made you think** so far…?

…and **why** did it do this?

What does a good argument look like?

10 second
summary

Rather than claiming something is true without justification, a good argument convincingly spells out *why* you ought to accept a claim: it answers the question **'why should I believe this?'**

Persuading people through reasoning

In everyday speech, an 'argument' means a disagreement (and may involve shouting). But when it comes to critical thinking, an argument is much more constructive than this: it's an attempt at **persuasion through reasoning**.

So far as thinking critically is concerned, every argument has two parts: its **conclusion**, which is the claim that you're being asked to believe; and its **premises**, which are a series of claims that together form a line of reasoning supporting the conclusion.

Evaluating and comparing the strengths of different arguments – and their weaknesses and limitations – is a fundamental thinking skill.

Logic and likelihood

A student told us...

'I hate arguing with people, so I didn't really see the point of studying arguments – until I realised it was about explaining the thinking behind your ideas. Then I started to get it.'

There are two ways in which you can use a line of reasoning to support a conclusion: by working through the **logical** consequences of things you believe to be true; and by working out the **likely** consequences of trends or patterns. This may sound complicated, but we do both of these things all the time:

Conclusion The endpoint of an **argument** – and thus the thing that whoever is making the argument wants to convince you of. An argument can only have one final conclusion. When assessing an argument, it's often best to identify the final conclusion and then work back from there.

- When we believe a claim is true, we work out what else must logically be true as well (*if all puppies need training, then any puppy I buy will need training*).

- When we spot a pattern or trend, we use it to work out what else is likely to be true (*a friend shakes my hand every time we meet: he's likely to do it again next time*).

The technical terms for these two types of reasoning are **deduction** and **induction**.

Introducing deduction

In a **deductive argument**, you set out your premises and then **deduce** what else must logically be true if your premises are true. What conclusion do you think follows logically here?

' I love all jazz piano music, and Oscar Peterson is a jazz pianist. So...'

The answer is that 'I must love the music of Oscar Peterson.' Here's this argument written in **standard form** – a clear, step-by-step way of presenting the key points in an argument:

Deductive reasoning
Reasoning that logically **deduces** a conclusion purely based on the content of premises. If the premises are true and the reasoning itself is logically **valid**, the conclusion must also be true – resulting in a **sound** argument. One problem with deductive reasoning is that people may use it to suggest a greater certainty than, in fact, is supported by reality.

PREMISE 1:   I love all jazz piano music.

PREMISE 2:   Oscar Peterson is a jazz pianist.

CONCLUSION: I love the music of Oscar Peterson.

If my premises are true and my logic is correct, my conclusion must also be true. If, however, either my logic is faulty or any of my premises are false, you can't trust my conclusion:

PREMISE 1:   I love all jazz piano music.

PREMISE 2:   Oscar Peterson is a jazz pianist.

CONCLUSION: I met Oscar Peterson once on holiday.

This introduces a new, irrelevant idea that doesn't logically follow from my claims.

Introducing induction

'You can only find truth with logic if you have already found truth without it.'

→ G K Chesterton

Instead of working out what must logically be true if our premises are true, an **inductive** argument makes a suggestion about what is likely to be true based on observations and generalisations. Imagine I say:

'I once met the jazz pianist Oscar Peterson, and he was very old. I bet all jazz pianists are very old!'

We can write this out in standard form:

PREMISE 1:   Oscar Peterson is very old.

PREMISE 2:   Oscar Peterson is a jazz pianist.

CONCLUSION: All jazz pianists are probably very old.

Is this convincing? No. Meeting one old jazz pianist doesn't tell me much about all jazz pianists. If I want to say something convincing about this, I'll need to gather more evidence.

Unlike a deductive argument, you can't judge an inductive argument simply by looking at its premises. You need to know something about the world – and whether what's being claimed is a fair generalisation, or only weakly supported by the evidence.

Inductive reasoning
Reasoning that suggests a **likely** conclusion on the basis of evidence and a general pattern. Good inductive reasoning gives us very strong reasons to accept that a conclusion is true, because it suggests an extremely plausible pattern based upon true premises. But induction can never actually prove a conclusion to be true with absolute certainty.

- **Good deductive arguments** correctly spell out logical conclusions based on true premises.

- **Good inductive arguments** convincingly spell out likely conclusions based on patterns and evidence.

CHECK POINT Types of reasoning

Match the definitions to the terms.

1 Inductive reasoning

2 Deductive reasoning

3 Conclusion

4 Premise

A The final claim that an argument is trying to persuade you of.

B Working out what is likely to be true on the basis of patterns and evidence.

C Working out what must, logically, be true if your initial claims are true.

D A claim that forms one step in an argument's line of reasoning.

What does a good explanation do?

10 second summary

A good explanation tries to offer the best possible account of how something came to be the way it is: it answers the question **'how did this happen?'**

The briefer the better

While an argument uses reasoning to try to draw out a convincing conclusion from its premises, **an explanation begins by assuming the truth of something** – then asks how this can most reasonably be explained.

A good explanation generally does two things. It manages to account for what you know (as opposed to ignoring whatever is inconvenient). And it manages to do this using as few steps as possible (as opposed to being unnecessarily complex).

The best explanation thus tends to be the simplest line of reasoning that still manages to explain all relevant evidence. This is sometimes known as the **principle of parsimony**.

Why, why, why?

A student told us...

'When people talked about research and hypotheses, my mind used to go blank. Now I see that it all comes down to explaining things – and how you can test your best ideas.'

We've said that a good explanation should:

1 Account for all the relevant information we know about something

2 Be as simple as possible while still explaining everything.

Let's look at a particular example.

You live with one housemate in a small flat. There are no guests staying with you and you bought milk yesterday – but now there's no milk in the fridge!

Which do you think is the best explanation?

A There's no milk in the fridge because your housemate used it all.

B There's no milk in the fridge because a neighbour sneaked in and drank it all.

C There is milk in the fridge, you're just not looking properly.

Explanation A good explanation should account for all the relevant evidence (rather than ignoring inconvenient facts) while being as simple as possible. A simple explanation is not guaranteed to be better than a complex one – but it is more likely to be true. This is known as the **principle of parsimony**.

A is the best of these explanations – because it accounts for everything without either introducing an unlikely new possibility (B) or implausibly denying certain facts (C).

Investigate!

At the same time, it should be clear that you can't be 100% sure A is correct. It certainly seems likely that your housemate used all the milk. But, before you adopt this as a definitive explanation, you may wish to conduct an **investigation**. It's possible that your housemate is innocent – and you don't want to accuse them wrongly.

There are two key questions that will help you investigate any explanation:

1   If your explanation is correct, what **predictions** can you make on its basis (and do these then come true)?

2   Does further investigation turn up any new evidence you can't explain – or suggest a plausible alternative explanation?

As you may have noticed, asking these questions turns even something as simple as wondering why you don't have any milk into a kind of research project. This is because research is at root a process of rigorously exploring explanations – and involves coming up with an explanation known as a **hypothesis** that can be tested against evidence.

> **Hypothesis** A prediction or proposed **explanation**, designed so that it can be tested by a **research process**. Rather than seeking confirmation, the best research tends to look for evidence with the potential to disprove a hypothesis, thus ensuring that it must pass a meaningful test.

Let's visualise the process…

- Initial fact-finding (*I bought milk yesterday, yet there's none in the fridge*).

- Developing a **hypothesis** about these facts (*my housemate drank it!*)

- Putting this hypothesis to a meaningful test (*I'm going to ask them if they did*).

- If necessary, repeating the process (*they swear they've hardly used any milk – so did one of us leave it somewhere else by mistake?*).

When you're wondering what a good explanation looks like, remember:

- You can never be 100% sure that any theory or explanation is correct, *but…*

- …the simplest theory that still explains everything is most likely to be true, *but…*

- …you need to make sure you've tested it by making predictions and looking for evidence, *and…*

- …you should always be ready to change your mind if the facts change.

CHECK POINT Explanations in practice

Look back over what you've read about explanations, then answer the following questions about my example of the housemate and the missing milk:

If I conduct a further investigation, one piece of evidence supporting the hypothesis that my housemate used all the milk would be ....

....

....

....

....

While a piece of evidence disproving this would be ....

....

....

....

....

'There is a sense in which we are all each other's consequences.'

Wallace Stegner

What about bad arguments and bad explanations?

10 second
summary

These rely upon dodgy hidden assumptions – or upon wrongly claiming that one thing must follow from another when it doesn't. Sometimes, this takes place behind a smokescreen of emotive language.

60 second
summary

The abuse of reasoning

The language of reasoning is often misused – for example, in the common claim that one thing *must* follow from another when, in fact, the real world is more complex.

We call an argument **fallacious** when its conclusion doesn't follow from its premises, or when it relies upon an unreasonable hidden assumption.

Most fallacies rely upon the fact that it's dangerously easy to deceive ourselves as well as others when it comes to things we *wish* were true.

Saying that someone *must* be wrong because of who they are is another common fallacy – and its simplicity, like most emotional manipulations, has a seductive appeal.

Too simple to be true

What's wrong with this line of argument?

We face a stark choice. On the one hand lies ruin at the hands of this incompetent government. On the other hand lies real change — which is why I deserve your vote!

The speaker wants you to agree with their conclusion (they deserve your vote) based on the reasoning that voting for them is the only alternative to ruin. Taken on its own terms, this sounds sensible. If it's true that there are only two options, and that one of these options leads to ruin, it does indeed make sense to vote for the other option.

As soon as we stop and think twice about this claim, however, it's clear that it involves this **unreasonable hidden assumption**:

Assumption Something relevant to a line of reasoning that has not been spelled out, but that the reasoning nevertheless depends upon. When writing out an argument in **standard form**, it's important to spell out clearly any assumption that the argument relies upon.

Standard form A usefully clear way of writing out the key ideas in an argument, step by step. Each **premise** should be clearly numbered in sequence, with the final **conclusion** at the very bottom. Using standard form is a great way to evaluate a line of reasoning.

There are only two possibilities, one of which is guaranteed to lead to ruin.

Does this accurately reflect the world? Almost certainly not. The speaker is establishing a **false dichotomy**, meaning that they are pretending that a complex situation can be reduced to a stark choice between two incompatible options.

Can you spot the unreasonable hidden assumption in this?

I have never heard the Prime Minister condemn physical punishment in schools. She's in favour of beating children!

The underlying problem is this assumption:

Unless something has definitively been proved to be false, we must assume that it's true.

This is a fallacy sometimes known as an **appeal to ignorance**, because it (wrongly) suggests that any lack of certainty about something automatically means that its opposite is true.

One useful way of testing a line of reasoning is to come up with a **comparable example**, using the same form of reasoning in a different context:

I have never heard my mother condemn alien invasions of Earth. She wants our planet to be taken over by creatures from outer space!

Fallacy An identifiable failure of reasoning, in which a line of reasoning that's claimed to be compelling turns out, on closer examination, to be faulty – usually because it relies upon a **faulty hidden assumption**. Common fallacies include **ad hominem** arguments, which attack a person rather than their ideas; and **non sequiturs**, which wrongly suggest that one thing must follow another.

Things to look out for

A student told us...

'Once you get in the habit of spotting bad reasoning, you start seeing it everywhere. The entire world is full of people pretending to be reasonable. Often, they honestly believe they're right.'

The best defence is to spell out other people's underlying assumptions – and never to assume that something must be true just because it's reasonable-sounding. In particular, watch out for:

- Someone judging a claim based upon *who* is saying it rather than its content.

- Someone saying that a complex situation can be reduced to a *simple choice.*

- Appeals to *tradition, emotion or authority* even when these aren't relevant.

- A *personal preference* or *anecdote* that has been dressed up as a general rule.

- The use of *distracting, confusing or emotional* language to hide a weak analysis.

Spot the assumptions

Can you spell out the unreasonable hidden assumption in these examples?

1   My father smoked every day of his life and lived to ninety. It can't be bad for you!

2   My physics tutor reckons rents in London will keep rising: I can't move there!

> 'When someone says his conclusions are objective, he means that they are based on prejudices which many other people share.'
>
> Celia Green

1   One individual case is a completely reliable guide to smoking's effects on health (it's not – we need to look at lots of cases to assess impacts on health).

2   A physics tutor has expert, reliable insights into London rents (no: unless we have reason to believe my tutor is a housing expert, their expertise is irrelevant).

Congratulations

You're getting to grips with **arguments and explanations.**

Can you think up a **faulty form of argument?**

...and then explain **what's wrong with it?**

Isn't everyone biased?

10 second summary

Everyone has their own perspective, **and there's no such thing as being perfectly unbiased** – but this only makes it more important to make our work as objective as possible.

Bias is a kind of blindness

Saying that someone is biased suggests they have a one-sided view of something that they ought to be more open-minded about.

By contrast, if you're trying to come up with an **objective** account, you need to take into account several different points of view and gather evidence widely.

Trying to see things objectively entails working out, as far as possible, what is actually going on. But it doesn't mean accepting that all perspectives are equally valid.

Objectivity is about carefully judging evidence and ideas, asking which are most reasonable – and not going along with whatever first comes to mind.

Better the bias you know

Conscious bias describes someone who is deliberately taking a one-sided view of something. We see this a lot in advertising and politics:

You should buy our car, it's the best in the world!

You shouldn't vote for her, she's the worst politician in history!

As long as you're aware that someone is likely to be biased – because, for example, they're selling something – it's relatively easy to engage with conscious bias. Here's a four-step process for dealing with issues about which people have very different views:

Bias Someone is said to be biased if their approach to something is misleadingly one-sided or based upon prejudice: a biased approach is one that ignores important evidence or ideas. **Conscious bias** is deliberate (such as an advertising slogan) while **unconscious bias** is something we don't notice (such as a preference for familiar faces). Contrast this to taking a more **objective** approach.

Objectivity An objective account is one that aims at eliminating **bias** and, as far as possible, describing the way that things actually are. There is no such thing as perfect objectivity, which is why being as objective as possible tends to entail a careful discussion of sources and research methods.

A student told us

'Everyone is biased, so you can't really prove anything. That's what I used to think. Then I realised it doesn't make sense. It's like saying, everyone has got some money – so there's no such thing as being rich.'

1 Make sure you have listened to all the different opinions involved (and that you understand each point of view).

2 Make sure you have identified the key relevant facts of the situation (and that you're satisfied these underlying facts are accurate).

3 Try to work out where the key disagreements lie (and what, if anything, the different sides agree upon).

4 Offer as objective a summary as possible by reporting the main differences in opinion, the key facts, and the points of agreement and disagreement.

By contrast, **unconscious bias** describes a situation in which someone has a distorted view of a situation for reasons that they're not even aware of. There are many different types of unconscious bias, but its most important and common effects include:

- **Confirmation:** people are more likely to seek out and pay attention to information that confirms their existing beliefs than they are to information that doesn't.

- **Availability**: people tend to attribute too much significance to things that they already know about, or that come easily to mind, compared to areas they know little about.

- **Framing:** all judgements are relative, which means that people are often excessively influenced by the context in which something is presented, even if this is misleading.

- **Affect**: people tend to confuse 'gut' emotional reactions with a valid judgement about whether something is bad or good – and thus to oversimplify complex questions.

In order to think well and conduct good research, try to avoid these traps by:

- Testing rather than seeking to confirm ideas.

- Deliberately going beyond what you already know.

- Trying out several different framings for questions and data.

- Setting aside your initial emotional responses.

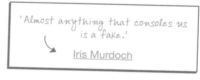

'Almost anything that consoles us is a fake.'

Iris Murdoch

Types of unconscious bias

Match each example to one of the effects of unconscious bias described above (Confirmation, Availability, Framing, Affect).

A Every time I look at a small child grasping a smartphone, a shiver goes down my spine. Those machines undermine our humanity.

B I've been to China at least once a year for the last decade, and I can unequivocally say that understanding China is the most important task for the world today.

C I'm the kind of person who hates fancy restaurants – and I can tell just by looking at the cover of this menu that I hate it.

D The most expensive wine on this menu is over a thousand dollars, which makes this $100 bottle a real bargain!

C – Confirmation / D – Framing
A – Affect / B – Availability /
Answers

How can I spot bias and misinformation?

10 second summary

Misinformation and half-truths are all around us – and seeing through them is about slowing down, thinking twice, and knowing how to confidently compare different sources.

60 second summary

Swimming in a sea of error

Misinformation is inaccurate or false information that may, or may not, be actively intended to fool you – but that can leave you deeply confused about what is going on.

Online misinformation can end up influencing seemingly reliable people and sources – which makes investigating the origins of a claim one of the most important tests of its accuracy.

When you come across a startling, unusual or strange claim – pause. Then to try to answer three questions:

'*What* am I being asked to believe;

How is this claim supported by evidence;

Where does this evidence originally come from?'

Spotting online misinformation in six steps

A student told us...

'People talk about fake news all the time, but often they just mean stories they don't like. It used to make me feel hopeless. Then I realised – you can track this stuff down, you can trace it, you can join the dots. You can beat the lies.'

It's important to be **sceptical** about any strange, unusual or surprising claims you come across – or anything that seems too good to be true. Scepticism simply means requiring further proof before you believe something, as opposed to automatically accepting it.

I've written the following guide specifically to help you practice scepticism online. But you can use its general principles across the rest of your life and work.

Misinformation Untrue or misleading information. Unlike **disinformation**, which is deliberately intended to deceive, misinformation isn't necessarily trying to fool you – it can simply be wrong because of confusion, error or ignorance. Dealing with misinformation entails pausing, evaluating evidence, comparing different sources, and investigating the origins of a claim.

ONE. What exactly is being claimed?
The first thing you need to do is work out what, exactly, you're being asked to believe. Try putting a headline or caption into your own words. Imagine you're explaining it to somebody else. What is going on?

TWO. Is what's being claimed shocking, extreme – or too good to be true? The more exceptional a claim is, the more exceptional the evidence supporting it needs to be. If something seems too good to be true, it probably is. Beware of manipulative clickbait.

THREE. Who is making this claim?
What's the source of the claim – and do you trust them? Look at some other stories from the same source. Does it have a good reputation? Have you heard of it before? Does the source of the story seem to have an agenda or bias?

> **Scepticism** Doubting the truth of something – as opposed to immediately accepting it as true. Practising a constructively sceptical attitude is essential for critical thinking, as it demands that you pause, think twice and ask what's really going on.

FOUR. Are they who they claim to be? Is the source you're dealing with what it claims to be? Look at the headline, the URL, the formatting. Are there errors or oddities, compared to sources you do trust? Search for the name of the source elsewhere. What comes up?

FIVE. What evidence is being used to support this claim? Where does the source link to? Is its evidence based upon named, reliable external sources – or are its claims vague and unsupported (or linked only to a network of 'friendly' sites)? Do the dates and images you're looking at check out – or have they been altered, or taken out of context?

SIX. Where does it fit into the big picture? This is worth asking about even the most reliable news stories. The best way to thinking critically about any story is to put it in a wider context – to see what else is being said in different places. If nobody else is writing about something, that's suspicious. *Compare, contrast, investigate.* Build your own understanding.

> 'Thinking is a form of feeling; feeling is a form of thinking.'
> Susan Sontag

How well do you know fake news? Copy out a headline, below, from a mainstream site.

....

....

....

Now try rewriting your own shockingly biased clickbait version of the same headline.

....

....

....

How can I handle information overload?

10 second summary

You can learn how to cope with information overload and make good use of technology – as long as you're prepared to **look closely at your own habits and assumptions.**

Beware of your own default settings

We use dozens of technologies every day, often without thinking about what we're doing: messages are constantly buzzing into our pockets, updates stream constantly past.

Making better use of technology involves two kinds of negotiation. First, you need to think actively about your own technological habits – and how to make the best use of your time.

Second, you need to think about the ways in which different technologies encourage you to behave – and how you ensure they're serving your needs as well as their manufacturers'.

Think of it as a careful adjustment of both your own and your devices' default settings!

The power of knowledge

'I can't remember the last time I was without my phone. I get anxious if I can't see it. I know that I need to find a way to slow down, online. I need to work through things at my own pace – and that means cutting out distractions.'

We looked in Section 2 at how you can establish priorities and create high quality time in your day. But what does it mean to think usefully about information itself? Remember:

- **Information** isn't the same thing as **knowledge.**

- Information describes all of the claims that are out there in the world…

- …while knowledge describes information you have good reason to believe is true.

In other words, there's a big difference between having access to information and being confident that you actually know what is going on. Consider this example:

The world's deepest ocean is the Pacific. It's over fifteen miles deep at its lowest point.

Is this knowledge, or just information? To answer this, you need to find out whether you have good reasons to accept it as true – a process known as **verification**.

Take a moment, right now, to investigate the claim above.

Start your search

Done? Assuming you did investigate this claim, I imagine you typed a query into a search engine: something like the three words *Pacific Deepest Ocean*. You'll then have seen a page of results and (probably) clicked on one of the top few, such as Wikipedia or Geology.com.

Both Wikipedia and Geology.com state that the deepest part of the world's oceans is the Mariana Trench, which lies in the Pacific Ocean and has been measured at its deepest point at 10,994m. You may also have noticed that 10,994m is (as a few more clicks on a search engine confirm) only around 6.8 miles.

Verification The process of working out whether something is true or not. This is how we turn **information** (a claim of any kind) into **knowledge** (a claim that we have good reasons to believe is true). Verification involves research – and being **transparent** about this process is important.

In other words, the information I provided was partly incorrect. As a result of a simple verification process, you now know with a reasonable degree of confidence that the Pacific ocean is indeed the world's deepest, and descends to almost 11,000m.

Do you know this with absolute certainty? No. In order to express knowledge as usefully and carefully as possible, we need to be **transparent** about how we've verified it – and what the limitations of this process were. After a little more investigation, we might say:

According to sources such as Wikipedia and Geology.com, the Mariana trench in the Pacific ocean is the deepest part of the Earth's oceans, with a depth of 10,994m (plus or minus 30m) recorded in a spot known as the Challenger Deep – although some one-off measurements have suggested possible depths of just over 11,000m.

Search, discover and be transparent

You need to get into the habit of handling information in this way. And this means practising a process of **search, discovery** and **transparency** that can help you turn information into knowledge – and research into understanding.

1 Conduct an initial **search** for key terms and ideas, allowing you to clarify exactly what is being claimed or investigated.

2 Follow this with a **discovery** process in which you explore the wider context of these claims, the origins of the information you're interested in, and the debate and challenges around it.

3 Use your discovery process to **unlock** further searches by following up on new keywords, claims, debates, sources and ideas you have discovered.

4 **Repeat** this process to keep on verifying and deepening your knowledge.

5 Finally, present a **transparent** account at the end in which you identify your sources and demonstrate your understanding.

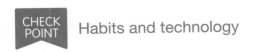

Habits and technology

What are your own best and worst everyday habits when it comes to technology?

One of my *best* tech habits is

....

And one of my *worst* tech habits is

....

What's going on in each of the cases above? What can you do differently?

....

....

....

....

....

> 'I don't think necessity is the mother of invention — invention, in my opinion, arises directly from idleness...'
>
> Agatha Christie

Congratulations

You're getting to grips with biases and tech habits.

Can you think of a bias you'd like to overcome?

....

...and a habit that might help you do this?

....

What do I do next?

*10 second
summary*

Critical thinking can be a powerful
positive force if you use it to reflect
on your habits, practices and ideas –
and try to stay flexible, open-minded
and willing to learn.

60 second
summary

This book is only the beginning

This final chapter contains questions that only you can answer. There are no right or wrong answers – only opportunities for exploring and clarifying what happens next.

What are your priorities? What are the habits and practices that will help you pursue them? What is holding you back? What can, and can't, you change?

We'll work through these and other questions in a structured way. Remember: **no answer need be final**. The more time you're able to spend thinking deeply about questions that matter, the better you'll be equipped to keep learning.

Keeping on thinking!

A student told us...

'I don't spend a lot of time asking myself questions. I'm always asking other people, or Google – but not me. So that's something I want to do. Take a little time, just for me, to work out what's happening in my head.'

You should recognize this quiz from the start of the book. Rate your confidence from one to ten in each of these categories, where one is least and ten is most confident.

1   I know what someone means when they talk about critical thinking. .... /10

2   I can make the time to think about things that matter. .... /10

3   I can offer good reasons for my own beliefs. .... /10

4   I can understand other people's reasoning. .... /10

5   I know what it means to explain something well. .... /10

6   I can tell the difference between good and bad reasoning. .... /10

7   I understand the ideas of bias and objectivity. .... /10

8   I'm good at spotting biased or inaccurate claims. .... /10

9   I'm confident doing online research and using
technology in my work. .... /10

10   I know what my priorities are for
learning and improving. .... /10

TOTAL .... /100

Reflect

How have your individual scores changed since you first answered these questions? What is your overall score now?

Even if you've only improved a little: congratulations. Well done for working through this book in the first place, for being honest, and for taking the time to think.

Based on your scores above, you may want to go back and carefully read through any sections for which your score is still less than five. Pay attention, too, to any area you don't think you've improved in.

Look ahead and make a plan

Now, no matter how you've done, it's time to look ahead and make a plan. Here's a structured way of helping you put some priorities, goals and reflections in place. Complete the following sentences in whatever way feels most honest and interesting to you:

The **first three things** I want to learn more about after finishing this book are:

1 ....

2 ....

3 ....

While in the **longer term** I want to learn about...

....

....

Three **good habits** that are going to help me keep on improving are:

1 ....

2 ....

3 ....

While I am going to try to spend less time...

As I thinker, I would describe myself as someone who.............................

....

And if there's one piece of advice I could give myself, it's.........................

....

....

'When I'm writing, I am trying to find out who I am, who we are, what we're capable of...'

Maya Angelou

Final checklist: How to know you are done

- [ ] I can tell the difference between critical and uncritical thinking

- [ ] I'm able to make the time to think twice about things that matter

- [ ] I know what it means to spell out my reasoning – and why this is useful

- [ ] I can spot when someone is using reasoning to support a conclusion

- [ ] I know what a good explanation ought to do

☐ I can evaluate someone else's reasoning – and look for false assumptions

☐ I know the difference between being biased and aiming at objectivity

☐ I've got a strategy for sniffing out misinformation

☐ I've got a strategy for coping with information overload

☐ I've started to think about the next steps I need to take to keep improving

Glossary

Argument   Using **reasoning**, in the form of a **premise** or linked **premises,** to try to persuade someone that they should accept the truth of a **conclusion.** An argument is thus an attempt at persuasion through reasoning.

Assertion   Something that, in contrast to the conclusion of an argument, is simply claimed to be true without any reasons being given in support. An assertion is often treated as self-evident, and thus requiring no justification, by the person who said it.

Assumption   Something relevant to a line of reasoning that has not been spelled out, but that the reasoning nevertheless depends upon. When writing out an argument in **standard form**, it's important to spell out clearly any assumption that the argument relies upon.

Bias   Someone is said to be biased if their approach to something is misleadingly one-sided or based upon prejudice: a biased approach is one that ignores important evidence or ideas. **Conscious bias** is deliberate (such as an advertising slogan) while **unconscious bias** is

something we don't notice (such as a preference for familiar faces). Contrast this to taking a more **objective** approach.

Conclusion   The end-point of an **argument** – and thus the thing that whoever is making the argument wants to convince you of. An argument can only have one final conclusion. When assessing an argument, it's often best to identify the final conclusion and then work back from there.

Deductive reasoning   Reasoning that logically **deduces** a conclusion purely based on the content of premises. If the premises are true and the reasoning itself is logically **valid**, the conclusion must also be true – resulting in a **sound** argument. One problem with deductive reasoning is that people may use it to suggest a greater certainty than, in fact, is supported by reality.

Explanation   A good explanation should account for all the relevant evidence (rather than ignoring inconvenient facts) while being as simple as possible. A simple explanation is not guaranteed to be better than a complex one – but it is more likely to be true. This is known as the **principle of parsimony**.

Fallacy   An identifiable failure of reasoning, in which a line of reasoning that's claimed to be compelling turns out, on closer examination, to be faulty – usually because it relies upon a **faulty hidden assumption**. Common fallacies include **ad hominem** arguments, which attack a person rather than their ideas; and **non sequiturs**, which wrongly suggest that one thing must follow another.

Hypothesis   A prediction or proposed **explanation**, designed so that it can be tested by a **research process**. Rather than seeking confirmation, the best research tends to look for evidence with the potential to disprove a hypothesis, thus ensuring that it must pass a meaningful test.

Inductive reasoning   Reasoning that suggests a **likely** conclusion on the basis of evidence and a general pattern. Good inductive reasoning gives us very strong reasons to accept that a conclusion is true, because it suggests an extremely plausible pattern based upon true premises. But induction can never actually prove a conclusion to be true with absolute certainty.

Misinformation   Untrue or misleading information. Unlike **disinformation**, which is deliberately intended to deceive, misinformation isn't necessarily trying to fool you – it can simply be wrong because of confusion, error or ignorance. Dealing with misinformation entails pausing, evaluating evidence, comparing different sources, and investigating the origins of a claim.

Objectivity   An objective account is one that aims at eliminating **bias** and, as far as possible, describing the way that things actually are. There is no such thing as perfect objectivity, which is why being as objective as possible tends to entail a careful discussion of sources and research methods.

Premise   In an argument, premises are the claims that support the **conclusion**. For an argument to succeed, its premises need to form a convincing line of reasoning. An argument can have only one premise – or many. The key point is that, taken together, they should demonstrate the conclusion is correct.

Principle of charity   The principle that you should engage with the strongest form of other people's ideas and arguments, rather than assuming they're wrong or misguided. This helps you learn as much as possible from others, and perhaps persuade them – as opposed to setting up a **straw man** in the form of a deliberately absurd misrepresentation of someone else's ideas.

Scepticism   Doubting the truth of something – as opposed to immediately accepting it as true. Practising a constructively sceptical attitude is essential for critical thinking, as it demands that you pause, think twice and ask what's really going on.

Standard form   A usefully clear way of writing out the key ideas in an argument, step by step. Each **premise** should be clearly numbered in sequence, with the final **conclusion** at the very bottom. Using standard form is a great way to evaluate a line of reasoning.

Verification   The process of working out whether something is true or not. This is how we turn **information** (a claim of any kind) into **knowledge** (a claim that we have good reasons to believe is true). Verification involves research – and being **transparent** about this process is important.

Further resources

Here are a range of resources to give you further help and support in order to think critically.

In print

Nigel Warburton's *Thinking from A to Z* (3rd Edition: New York, 2007). Offers a short, sharp tour of key words and ideas in critical thinking.

Walter Sinnott-Armstrong's *Think Again: How to Reason and Argue* (London, 2018). Makes an elegant case for the significance of reasoning today.

Dan Ariely's *Predictably Irrational* (London, 2009). A fine foundational guide to modern research into human irrationality, bias and behavioural impulses.

Jaron Lanier's *You Are Not A Gadget* (London, 2010). Although it's been around for a while in tech terms, this remains a hugely engaging impetus for thinking critically about technology.

If you've enjoyed this book, my own *Critical Thinking: Your Guide to Effective Argument, Successful Analysis & Independent Study* (London, 2018) greatly expands on its ideas.

Online

The *Philosophy Bites* podcast is one of the richest yet most accessible listening resources around for exploring the ideas of world-leading thinkers in their own words.

The *Stanford Encyclopaedia of Philosophy* is a free, extensive and expertly maintained online resource for thinking about thinking – best enjoyed by diving into an entry at random.

If you want an insight into one of the most important battlegrounds for modern knowledge, get into the habit of clicking on 'view history' to look into the edit history behind different *Wikipedia* articles – especially those you know something about. Once you've got the hang of things, see if you can find ways to improve the quality of entries by editing them yourself.

You can use technology to carve out some interrupted thinking time via tools like the anti-distraction app Freedom, which can be set to selectively disable internet connectivity.

Or you could just turn your phone off and go for a walk.